PIE
CONTEST
IN A BOX
Handbook

PIE
CONTEST
IN A BOX
Handbook

EVERYTHING YOU NEED TO HOST A PIE CONTEST

**Andrews McMeel
Publishing, LLC**
Kansas City • Sydney • London

Andrews McMeel Publishing, LLC
an Andrews McMeel Universal company
1130 Walnut Street, Kansas City, Missouri 64106

www.andrewsmcmeel.com

11 12 13 14 15 LEO 10 9 8 7 6 5 4 3 2 1

ISBN: 978-1-4494-0101-6

ATTENTION: SCHOOLS AND BUSINESSES

Andrews McMeel books are available at quantity discounts with bulk purchase for educational, business, or sales promotional use. For information, please e-mail the Andrews McMeel Publishing Special Sales Department: specialsales@amuniversal.com

For the pie queens in my family:
my mother-in-law, Babs Barrett,
and my grandmother, Mae Augusta Nickerson.

CONTENTS

CHAPTER SIX

Pie Tunes Playlist, Children's Books About Pie, and
Great Pie Fights in Movie History ✳ 83

INTRODUCTION

WHY PIE MATTERS TODAY

Pie makes people happy. Happy people want to do nice things for others.
When everyone is doing nice things for each other all the time
there can be no war, and therefore pie can save the world.

Beth Howard, apple pie baker

EVERY PIE TELLS A STORY OF HOME.

Queen Esther, who won the award for Best Savory Pie at the 2010 Roaring '20s Jazz Age Lawn Party Pie Contest on New York's Governors Island, explains, "Instinctively [when you eat pie], you are reaching for your idea of what home is—and for that comfort—with every bite, even if you didn't have a mother and a grandmother and a great-grandmother that baked, like I did, or even if home for you was a negative situation." In these high-tech, high-stress times, the simple grace of pie is needed more than ever. Pie contests are a way for families and communities to unite on common ground. You might fight about politics or religion, but everyone agrees that pie is good.

* * *

When you start talking pie, faces light up. When you invite someone to be a pie judge, a Cheshire cat–like grin is the usual response. Everyone, it seems, secretly wants to be a pie judge. Even people who don't realize it's their life's ambition to judge pie are thrilled by the request. I recently tested my theory that anyone will agree to be a pie judge by inviting several winners of the MacArthur "genius awards" ($500,000 grants given by the John D. and Catherine T. MacArthur Foundation) to be judges at the Hancock Shaker Village Country Fair Pie Contest in Pittsfield, Massachusetts. The geniuses replied immediately and with delight. One scientist from Harvard said it was about the nicest invitation he'd ever received.

* * *

My point is that you can think strategically and aim high with your pie judge invitations. Who do you want to know, curry favor with, or honor? The handsome guy you always see at the dog park? The owner of a local business you'd like to work for someday? A dedicated volunteer or donor who supports your favorite nonprofit organization? The only required qualification is that they love pie, and anyone worth knowing loves pie. (As singer-songwriter Aimee Mann says, "You have to admit there is something about the texture of pie that is a lot sexier than cake. Cake is merely a square of sweet.")

❄ ❄ ❄

Pie levels the playing field. It doesn't need to be expensive to win blue ribbons. You don't need fancy equipment—just a bowl, a rolling pin, a paring knife, a whisk or wooden spoon, a pie pan, and perhaps some dried beans to use as pie weights. Some bakers swear by food processors to make crust and those French ceramic pie pans with the scalloped edges are charming and you can spend a small fortune on eBay collecting vintage pie birds (ceramic steam vents shaped like birds), not to mention all the fabulous retro aprons available these days. But none of those things is really important, and you don't need gourmet or exotic ingredients, either. The best pies are often made of the simplest fresh ingredients, the most important of which is love. You just need to practice. A great thing about learning to bake is that even the most horrific-looking beginner pies tend to taste good.

❄ ❄ ❄

Pie inspires good times, good will, and a sense of community. I hope that *Pie Contest in a Box*, with its prize ribbons, judge badges, pie toppers, scorecards, blue ribbon–winning recipes, and pie songs, will lead to a happy day for you and yours . . . and that it will contribute, in its own little way, to world peace.

CHAPTER ONE

A Brief History of Pie

The evolution of human food goes something like this: First our ancestors hunted and gathered, and then they invented pie. It is one of the most ancient foods, seemingly baked into our collective DNA since the dawn of civilization.

* * *

The first known pies can be traced back to the Egyptians. The bakers to the pharaohs made free-form meat pies. They invented a hard, inedible crust of oats, wheat, rye, and barley around 9500 BC during the Neolithic period. These crusts were made several inches thick to withstand hours of baking over hot coals, and they served as both a baking dish and as an airtight method of preservation, sort of like the original Tupperware.

* * *

Pie spread from Egypt to Greece to Rome, and eventually throughout all of Europe. The ancient Greeks invented a water-flour paste pie crust that they wrapped like homemade tinfoil around meat to seal in juices as it cooked. These lightweight, portable pies were handy on long sea journeys, as the crust helped keep the meat from spoiling. The ancient Romans made pielike puddings of lampreys, oysters, and mussels. They also made temple offerings to their gods of a pie called *libum*, which consisted of flour dough sheets topped with cheese and honey and flavored with bay leaves.

* * *

During medieval times, animated pies (spelled "pyes") were all the rage as entertainment at royal feasts. These pies contained live birds, frogs, turtles,

rabbits, and sometimes even poetry-reciting dwarfs. The nursery rhyme "Sing a Song of Sixpence" refers to this genre of delicacy with its "four-and-twenty blackbirds baked in a pie." As the rhyme explains, "When the pie was opened, the birds began to sing. Wasn't that a dainty dish to set before the king?" In 1454, the French Duke of Burgundy is said to have been delighted at the Feast of the Pheasant when his chef baked an enormous pie that opened to the strains of a small orchestra playing from inside. According to Janet Clarkson in her book, *Pie: A Global History*, pie crusts during this period were called "coffins" or "coffyns" (meaning "basket" or "box," not an accessory for cannibalism).

※ ※ ※

The Renaissance, with its focus on art and innovation, brought about the more mild-mannered and refined pies we know today. Northern Italian bakers started mixing butter into their pastry dough, French chefs embraced the art of fruit tarts, and British cooks introduced lard to their pork-pie crusts. British legend has it that Queen Elizabeth I herself invented cherry pie, though it seems unlikely that she spent much time in the kitchen.

※ ※ ※

The Pilgrims brought pie with them to the New World in 1620, and adapted their family recipes to the local environment. They used the berries and fruits (most famously pumpkin) that the Native Americans showed them and incorporated new ingredients, such as eggs and molasses.

※ ※ ※

Pioneer women in the 1700s often served pie for breakfast, lunch, and dinner, thus establishing the pastry as the sentimental heart of American family gatherings. George Washington was known to be especially fond of sweetbreads pie. Pie-baking and pie-eating contests, along with pie-throwing games, became the focal point of county fairs, picnics, and other community celebrations, and these traditions continue to this day.

* * *

As John Lehndorff of the American Pie Council explains, "When you say that something is 'as American as apple pie,' what you're really saying is that the item came to this country from elsewhere and was transformed into a distinctly American experience." Love of the many splendored thing called pie, however, knows no borders. While people in the United States typically favor sweet flavors, pie-crazy Australians, Canadians, New Zealanders, and residents of the United Kingdom are passionate about their savory varieties—from chicken and mushrooms to steak, kidney, and mutton. In the Caribbean, macaroni pie is considered traditional West Indian comfort food. Coconut pies are popular in Liberia and Tanzania, milk custard ones in South Africa, and miniature chicken pot pies are a favorite Chinese dim sum dish.

* * *

Pie endures. Its perfect form of crust and filling transcends time and place, connecting us to our ancestors and to our shared humanity.

CHAPTER TWO

Anatomy of a Pie Contest

*I believe most home cooks bake a pie because they want to
engage their senses, do something that's tactilely rewarding.
Pie is a craft, after all, and one we can be proud of.
Indeed, one of the most satisfying things about making pie
is showing it off just a little, then sharing what we've created.*

Ken Haedrich, cookbook author
. . . .

If you bake them, they will come.

Anne Dimock, pie memoirist
. . . .

ADVANCE PLANNING

Choose your date and time and decide what sort of theme you want for your pie contest. See chapter 3 for theme suggestions ranging from single-category contests (that is, everyone makes the same type of pie) to pie contests that celebrate family heirloom recipes or that double as costume parties.

Figure out whom you'd like to judge your pie contest and invite them. There are five pie judge badges in this kit.

Once you've secured your judges, announce your contest, including the judges' names and affiliations as appropriate, along with the date, time, place, theme, entry fee if you're going to charge one, and RSVP information.

On your invitation, tell pie contest entrants what time they should deliver their pies. This kit is designed for up to twelve competitors; a half hour before the judging is set to begin is sufficient. If you are expecting significantly more entrants (like at the American Pie Council Crisco National Pie Championships, where two hundred judges evaluate more than one thousand pies!), then allow yourself more time to register and organize the pies. Also, ask the contestants to bring a knife and pie spatula to help serve their pies (unless your home is already well stocked with these implements).

SETTING THE STAGE

A Note about Supplies

Pie contests require lots of small plates, forks, knives, and napkins. Disposable paper and plastic products are most convenient, but please consider ecological alternatives, such as plates and cutlery made of recycled and/or biodegradable material and cloth napkins. This kit is designed for five judges judging twelve pies, which

adds up to sixty plates and forks for the judging table; plus, you'll need one plate and fork for each of your guests to sample all the pies in order to vote for People's Choice. If you don't happen to own that many plates and forks, consider asking your friends to bring their own to the party, or rent supplies from a catering company.

On the big day, set each place at the judging table with a glass for water, a small plate, fork, napkin, pen or pencil, and scorecards. If you're using disposable paper products, station a trash receptacle nearby.

❄ ❄ ❄

Set an official place for yourself at the judging table as well. You will need a knife and pie spatula, a water pitcher or other container that can be filled with warm water to clean implements between entries, and paper or tea towels to dry them off.

❄ ❄ ❄

In the middle of the judging table, place a stack of small plates, containers of forks and knives, extra napkins, and a pitcher of water. You will also need a calculator for adding up the scorecards. Optional: A dish of bland crackers for the judges to cleanse their palates with between tastings is a nice touch.

❄ ❄ ❄

Designate a side table (or a mixture of card tables and windowsills— whatever you've got) as the place to display the pies.

On one side of the pie-display area, set plates, forks, and napkins, and on the other side, create your People's Choice Voting Center. The ballot box can be a shoebox, basket, jar, or hat. Stock the voting area with pens or pencils and little pieces of paper to use as ballots.

❋ ❋ ❋

Use the tally sheet on the last page of this handbook to register each pie when the contestants arrive, designating a number for each entry in order to keep the baker's name anonymous during the judging.

❋ ❋ ❋

Fill in the title of each pie on the numbered pie topper that corresponds to the entry and immediately place it in the pie lest you get confused. "Classic Sweet Potato Pie" is a fine name, but "Put a Smile on My World Gooseberry Pie" and "Lemon Cloud Pie in the Sky" are more fun. Encourage your contestants to be creative with their pie titles.

❋ ❋ ❋

If you have more than twelve contestants, continue your tally sheet on a separate piece of paper and use index cards instead of pie toppers to identify the pies by number and title.

❋ ❋ ❋

When the judges arrive, bestow upon them their official pie judge badges. Use safety pins or tape to affix the badges to the judges' clothing.

LET THE JUDGING BEGIN

* Start the proceedings by reading aloud the brief essay "The Zen of Judging Pie," which is located on page 21 of this handbook.

* Announce the name and number of each pie when you bring it to the judging table. Instruct the judges to note these details on their scorecards.

* First present the pie whole for the judges to rate its first impression, then cut one slice so they can judge how it holds up on a plate.

* Once the judges are done rating the pie's appearance, send the slice around the judging table with a small knife for the judges to each cut a sliver for themselves that contains both crust and filling.

* The judges will then rate the crust, filling, and overall impressions of the pie.

* Conversation between the judges is welcome, but they should keep their individual scores private.

* When the judges finish evaluating each pie, they should total their scorecards. Pass the calculator around the table as needed.

* Collect the scorecards and give them to an assistant to go off to a corner and total the combined judges' score for each pie.

✳ Clear the used plates and forks between entries. If you've decided to go super eco-friendly and use real plates and cutlery, have two sets on hand and ask an assistant to wash and dry one set while the other is in use at the judging table.

✳ After all of the pies have been judged, enter the various score totals onto the tally sheet on the last page of this handbook. Determine which pies won first, second, and third prize.

✳ Now it's time for the people to have their say. Everyone at the party should taste all of the pies and vote for their favorite to win the People's Choice Award. To vote for a pie, write its entry number on the ballot. Every person gets one vote, and bakers may vote for their own pies if they really think they are the best.

✳ Once everyone has participated, take the ballot box to a corner or separate room and tally up the People's Choice votes.

✳ Drum roll, please. . . . When you're ready to announce the winners, gather everyone together and award the prize ribbons starting with third place, then second, then first, and lastly, People's Choice. Read aloud the judge's comments about each winning pie.

✳ Ta-da!

CHAPTER THREE

Pie Contest Themes

OPEN PIE CONTEST

Contestants are free to enter their favorite pie, whatever it may be.

SINGLE INGREDIENT OR CATEGORY PIE CONTEST

Choose a single ingredient (mango, molasses, mutton, and so forth) or category of pie (such as berry, cookie, cream, custard, fruit, icebox, nut, savory, or vegan).

SEASONAL PIE CONTEST

Invite contestants to celebrate the flavors of the season.

SPRING: lemon, mango, rhubarb, strawberry

SUMMER: apricot, blackberry, blueberry, boysenberry, cherry, fig, gooseberry, nectarine, peach, plum, raspberry

FALL: apple, cranberry, pear, pumpkin, sweet potato

WINTER: chocolate, eggnog, kiwi, mincemeat, pecan, tangerine, walnut, winter squash

FARMERS' MARKET PIE CONTEST

Make pies using ingredients from your local farmers' market.

HARD-CORE LOCAVORE

This theme takes the notions of local and seasonal foods one step further. Entrants are encouraged to see how local they can go, using homegrown or locally foraged ingredients—eggs from their backyard chicken coops, cream from cows they've personally milked, hand-churned butter, and the like.

FAMILY HEIRLOOM RECIPES PIE CONTEST

Invite entrants to bake their favorite family heirloom pie recipes and share stories of the loved ones who passed them down through the generations.

SEMI-HOMEMADE PIE CONTEST

Store-bought crusts allowed.

REGIONAL SPECIALTY PIE CONTEST

Focus your pie contest around a regional specialty, such as Southern Chess Pie, Pennsylvania Dutch Pie, Tropical Fruit Pie, or English Meat Pie.

BOOZE PIES PIE CONTEST

Make pies that incorporate alcohol. Think Whiskey and Buttermilk Pie, Slug-o-Bourbon Spiced Apple Pie, Kahlúa Fudge Brownie Pie, and Wine-Soaked Plums and Chèvre Pie.

PIES THAT ARE NOT REALLY PIES PIE CONTEST

While it's common knowledge that for a dish to be considered pie, it needs to have a pastry crust, there are many culinary creations called "pie" that don't fit this definition. Pie is a big tent. Consider hosting an inexplicable pie contest of pies that aren't really pies, such as Eskimo Pie (ice cream), Whoopie Pie (cake), Moon Pie (graham crackers and marshmallow fluff), Boston Cream Pie (cake), Cheesecake (which is pretty much pie), or Cow Pie (not seriously recommended).

PIE CONTEST **INSPIRED BY THE MOVIE _WAITRESS_**

In Adrienne Shelly's 2007 movie _Waitress_, Keri Russell plays a diner waitress stuck in a lousy marriage whose only solace is baking pies. She names her pies after the tumultuous events and emotions in her daily life, such as Kick in the Pants Pie (cinnamon spice custard), Baby Screaming Its Head Off in the Middle of the Night and Ruining My Life Pie (New York–style cheesecake, brushed with brandy and topped with pecans and nutmeg), and I Can't Have No Affair Because It's Wrong and I Don't Want Earl to Kill Me Pie (vanilla custard with banana; hold the banana). Invite your baker friends to express their sorrows in the form of a pie.

TURDUCKEN-STYLE PAKE PIE CONTEST

Throw a pie contest based on the growing, if somewhat disturbing, trend of baking pies inside of cakes.

WOMEN'S LIB UGLY PIES PIE CONTEST

If the 1950s were the Golden Age of American Pies, when housewives donned charming aprons and slaved away in the kitchen all day making coconut cream and lemon chiffon pies to please their hardworking husbands, the late 1960s and early 1970s era, with its liberated women and tie-dyed muumuus, was the

Dark Age of Pie. Working mothers created spectacularly ugly pies with store-bought crusts, gelatin flavors only vaguely rooted in nature, canned fruit, and artificial whipped topping. Dig out the vintage recipe pamphlets and see who can make the ugliest pie. Period costumes encouraged.

TOTALLY-NOT-MADE-FROM-SCRATCH "SPEED BAKING" PIE CONTEST

This pie contest is inspired by an *Iron Chef*–style one that Mary "Pie Lady" Pint, of American Blue Ribbon Holdings, hosts at the Great American Pie Festival each year. In this contest, teams of bakers collaborate using ready-made ingredients to create pies based on different themes, such as states (think Maine Pie adorned with a lighthouse made of blueberries), holidays (such as Easter Pie decorated with marshmallow peeps and chocolate eggs), and imaginary family crests (a fun theme for family reunions). To throw this contest, stock a table with precooked crusts for each team, bowls filled with various premixed and canned pudding and fruit fillings, nuts, raisins, candy, fresh fruit, chocolate and caramel sauce, and so on. Have your guests divide into teams, announce your theme, and then give them thirty minutes to create their masterpieces.

APHRODISIACS PIE CONTEST

In her book *Shakespeare's Kitchen*, food historian Francine Segan describes a popular Elizabethan dish called Courage Pie. This savory English concoction was intended to aid sexual prowess. It contained ingredients thought to be aphrodisiacs at the time, including sweet potatoes, quinces, dates, wine, rosewater, and always-sexy sparrow's brains. For this pie contest, entrants are charged with making pies that either contain traditional aphrodisiacs, such as chocolate, almonds, figs, honey, nutmeg, or pomegranates, or with ingredients that they personally have firsthand knowledge as being the way to their lovers' hearts.

PIE CONTEST AS HEALING FORCE

Master baker and teacher Kate McDermott sometimes dedicates her pies to friends in need. She says, "You can be spiritual and pray in whatever way you want. For me, I guess, it's pies and baking. My tagline is 'Making the world a better place, one pie at a time.' This is one small act I can do to try and send out good energy. If more people do it, pretty soon we may have made a difference in some way, even if it is to bring a smile to a face." Host a pie contest where everybody bakes their pie in honor of someone in your community who is struggling—whether they are facing cancer or unemployment or going through a difficult divorce—and invite that person to be the guest of honor at your party. If they are dealing with financial challenges, charge an entry fee and give the honoree the proceeds.

PIE-EATING CONTEST

Perhaps you bought this kit thinking that it was for a pie-*eating* contest, rather than a baking one. Rules for those sorts of contests vary, but the gist is that contestants compete to see who can eat the most pie the fastest without using their hands. You can specify that hands be sat upon or placed behind backs. Typically the pies served are identical; you can give each contestant either a whole pie or an individual slice to tackle. Please remind everyone to chew and swallow.

CHAPTER FOUR

I may not be able to define a pie, but I know one when I see it.

Raymond Sokolov, food scholar

. . . .

Judging pie is not an altogether rational activity. You bring to the table a life-time of pie experiences and associations. Some of your reactions will be objective, such as assessing that a crust is soggy or golden brown, but others will be more mysterious. You may find that your heart suddenly skips a beat when the taste of a certain peach pie transports you back to your first summer romance. A ginger snap cookie crust might prompt a wistful mood as it triggers the memory of your kind ex-father-in-law whom you never get to see anymore. As a judge, though, you need to set aside your personal biases as best you can and try to evaluate each pie on its own terms with an open mind and heart.

❄ ❄ ❄

Give the pie your full attention. Awaken all of your senses. Look at the pie, smell it, touch it, taste it, and listen to it. Pace yourself by taking small bites. Savor them in your mouth a little longer than usual in order to take in the nuances of flavor and texture. Let the pie tell you its story.

❄ ❄ ❄

"Do not get too infatuated with the first few pies," advises veteran pie judge Lesley Ann Beck. "Don't set the bar too high at the outset; a really spectacular entry might be coming along toward the end of the contest and there needs to be room to move it to the top of the list. Just like the Olympics."

First you will judge the pie's appearance. Prizewinning pies make a seductive first impression. The most beautiful pies are not necessarily the most uniformly perfect ones. The best pies, whether rustic or elegant, project authentic character and a clear sense of purpose. They aim to please.

Next you will take a bite of filling and then a bite of the crust to consider the merits of each element on its own before indulging in a combined bite. Fancy decorative crust treatments, such as cookie-cutter leaves, hearts, and stars, can delight, but they aren't worth much if they don't taste good. Crusts should be tender, flaky, and flavorful, and they should be thoroughly cooked, or done. "Doneness" is the technical term. Crusts need to hold up to the filling, which should be juicy, gooey, and delicious, not gritty, runny, or dry. The filling flavors must sing with freshness, strength, and balance.

The synthesis of crust and filling, however, is where the magic happens. Champion pies are greater than the sum of their parts. When you taste the composite elements together, ponder how the pie represents its category. Will you remember this pie? Does it embody the quintessential ideal of pieness? Have fun, and please remember to chew with your mouth closed and use a napkin to wipe away any pie that ends up on your face.

CHAPTER FIVE

Blue Ribbon Pie Recipes, and Tips, from the Champion Bakers,

Allison Kave **Brooklyn, New York**

Food has always been an integral part of Allison's family life. Her mother is a chocolatier, and her brother is a chef. She first started baking pie in her early teens and loved the process of baking, especially the meditative quality of working with dough—how you can't rush it and have to have the right ingredients and temperatures. She also found the physicality of baking to be soothing and uniquely satisfying. Soon, pie became her go-to dessert. After a decade-long career in the fine-arts world working as a curator, writer, and gallery director, she won the First Annual Brooklyn Pie Bake-Off, which inspired her to become a professional baker and open her own pie company, First Prize Pies.

Allison's Pie Contest Tips: "Don't get caught up in the competition aspect—just have fun with it! It's really an excuse for a community to get together, eat yummy treats, and get to know each other. In terms of your entry, make something you love, or something you've always wanted to try."

BOURBON GINGER PECAN PIE

by Allison Kave

Best Overall Pie Award Winner at the First Annual Brooklyn Pie Bake-Off in 2009

CRUST

Makes two 9-inch crusts (freeze the extra one for your next pie)

* 1½ cups unbleached all-purpose flour
* ½ cup cake flour
* 1 tablespoon kosher salt
* 1 tablespoon sugar
* 1½ sticks (12 tablespoons) unsalted butter plus 4 tablespoons leaf lard, chilled and diced, or 1 cup (2 sticks) unsalted butter, chilled and diced (see Tip on next page)
* ½ teaspoon white vinegar (if using lard)
* ½ cup very cold water

FILLING

* 1 cup firmly packed dark brown sugar
* 3 tablespoons unsalted butter, melted
* ½ cup maple syrup
* 3 large eggs, beaten
* 2 cups pecans, lightly toasted
* 2 or 3 tablespoons good bourbon
* Pinch of salt
* 1 teaspoon ground dried ginger
* 2 teaspoons (about a 2-inch piece) fresh ginger, peeled and finely grated (a Microplane grater is great for this)
* ¼ cup crystallized ginger, finely chopped

Tip: Leaf lard is really the best thing for pies, if you can find it. I buy it already rendered from my local farmers market, and you can often find it frozen at good food markets. If you do not want to use lard (although I recommend it as it makes an amazing crust), just replace it with butter and omit the white vinegar from the recipe. I'm not a fan of shortening, but you could substitute that if you want to.

Make the crust. I use a food processor for this, and it turns out wonderfully.

✳ ✳ ✳

In the work bowl of a food processor fitted with a metal blade, pulse the flours, salt, and sugar, just to combine. Add the butter and lard, and pulse a few times to cut the fat into the flour. The mixture should resemble coarse crumbs. Combine the vinegar with the water. With the processor running, pour the liquid down the feed tube all at once. As soon as the dough begins to form a ball around the blade, stop the machine. Lay a piece of plastic wrap on the counter and dump the dough onto it, scraping the bowl and blade with a spatula. Pat the dough into a ball, wrap lightly, and chill for at least an hour before using. At this point, dough can be refrigerated for up to 2 days or frozen for up to 2 months.

✻ ✻ ✻

After the dough has rested, lightly dust a clean work surface with flour, and roll out to a circle approximately 10 inches in diameter and about ⅛ inch thick. Line a 9-inch buttered pie plate with the dough and trim the overhang to about ½ inch. Do not prick with a fork. Tuck the overhang under the edge between the pie plate and the crust, and make a nice decoration around the edge by pinching the dough between your thumb and forefinger. Return the crust to the refrigerator to chill for another 20 to 30 minutes.

✻ ✻ ✻

Preheat the oven to 425°F. Line the crust with aluminum foil and fill with pie weights, dried beans, or dried rice to help the crust hold its shape while baking. Bake for 12 minutes, then remove the weights and foil, and return the crust to the oven for 10 more minutes, until it begins to brown lightly. Remove the crust from the oven and let it cool before filling. If the crust has bubbled up at all on the bottom don't worry, just lightly press down any bubbles.

✻ ✻ ✻

Turn the oven down to 350°F. While the crust cools, make the filling.

✻ ✻ ✻

In a mixing bowl, stir together the sugar and the melted butter. Add the maple syrup, eggs, pecans, bourbon, salt, and gingers, and stir until all ingredients are combined. Pour the mixture into the cooled pie crust, and bake for 25 to 35 minutes, until the pie is set. Remove the pie from the oven and cool it on a wire rack.

* * *

The pie can be frozen after it has cooled. To do so, wrap it well in plastic wrap and then foil or a freezer bag. The pie will keep for up to 2 months. Let it defrost at room temperature a few hours before serving.

Shannon Seath Meyer **Vashon, Washington**

Shannon lives on Vashon Island, a fifteen-minute ferry ride from Seattle, with her husband, two young daughters, her mother, and a yellow Labrador retriever named Teak. She describes herself as an "extreme homemaker," cooking most of her family's meals with food she grows in her garden, knitting, sewing, and keeping the house in running (if, she jokes, not terribly clean) order. She started baking in her early teens but didn't become a pie fan until she met her husband, who loves pumpkin pie. She asked friends and relatives for tips and says that each year, little by little, her pumpkin pie got better. Her mother, though, was the ultimate judge of the crust, comparing it to her Aunt Elsie's pie crust, the memory of which had achieved mythic status in the family. Elsie was a daily baker, who kept her flour in a ten-gallon tub and rendered her own lard. The day Shannon produced a crust that her mother said was as good as her Great-Aunt Elsie's, she knew she had a winner.

Shannon's Pie Contest Tips: "I have two tips. The first is don't get too fancy and add additional flavors. Your pumpkin pie should taste like pumpkin, say, not ginger or bourbon. The second tip is to perfect your crust. I have played and played with recipes, pans, and oven temperatures to get a nice flaky crust that is done just right."

TRADITIONAL PUMPKIN PIE
by Shannon Seath Meyer

Winner of First Prize—Traditional Pumpkin Pie at the 2009
Vashon Island Farmers Market Pumpkin Pie Taste-off

CRUST

*Makes two 9-inch crusts (freeze the extra one for
your next pie)*

* 2½ cups unbleached all-purpose
  flour
* 2 tablespoons sugar
* 2 teaspoons salt
* 1 cup (2 sticks) unsalted butter,
  chilled and diced
* ¼ cup ice water, or more as needed

CUSTARD

* 1⅔ cups fresh pumpkin puree
  (see Tip)
* ⅔ cup sugar
* ½ teaspoon salt
* 1 teaspoon cinnamon
* 1 teaspoon ground dried ginger
* ½ teaspoon allspice
* ¼ teaspoon ground cloves
* 1¼ cups heavy cream
* 3 eggs

Tip: I grow sugar pie pumpkins for my pumpkin pies. To make fresh pumpkin puree, preheat the oven to 400°F. Slice a pumpkin in half and scoop out the seeds and pulp. Place each half, cut side down, in a shallow pan (such as a 13 by 9-inch baking pan). Use two pans if needed. Fill each pan with about an inch or so of water. Bake for 40 to 60 minutes, depending on the size of the pumpkin, until the flesh is soft and a fork slides in easily. Check periodically to add more water if necessary. Carefully remove the pumpkin pieces from the water and let cool. When they are cool enough to handle, pull the rind off the flesh or scoop the flesh out of the rind. Puree flesh in a food processor. Store in the refrigerator until use or freeze for up to 3 months.

To make the crust, combine the flour, sugar, and salt. Cut the butter into the flour mixture with a pastry blender, food processor, or your fingers. (I use the last method, mixing the butter around the flour with my fingertips and then quickly smooshing each little butter lump between my fingers and thumb. This produces little lenses of butter that, I think, make a flakier crust. It is time consuming compared with the other methods, but I think it is worth it.) When the mixture resembles coarse crumbs, add as much water as needed to make a soft dough; it should stick together but not be sticky. Divide the dough into 2 balls and flatten each into a disc. Wrap the discs in plastic wrap or place in freezer bag. Freeze one for your next pie and set the other in the fridge to rest for at least an hour. At this point, dough can be refrigerated for up to 2 days or frozen for up to 2 months.

* * *

After the dough has rested, lightly dust a clean work surface with flour, and roll out your dough a bit larger than your pan. Gently place the dough in the pan and roll or crimp your edges around.

* * *

Preheat the oven to 400°F. Line the crust with aluminum foil and fill with pie weights, dried beans, or dried rice to help the crust hold its shape while baking. Bake for 10 to 15 minutes then remove the weights and foil, and return the crust to the oven for 5 to 10 more minutes, until the crust is a light tan color. Your oven and pie pan make this step variable, so check often. Tin plates brown much faster and ceramic is much slower. I use a Pyrex pie plate.

* * *

Remove the crust from the oven and let it cool before filling. If the crust has bubbled up at all on the bottom don't worry, just lightly press down any bubbles.

* * *

Turn the oven down to 350°F. While the crust cools, make the custard.

34

*   *   *

Combine the pumpkin puree, sugar, salt, cinnamon, ginger, allspice, and cloves in a saucepan or small soup pot and cook over medium heat, stirring often, to cook off some of the excess water and concentrate the flavors, about 10 minutes. The mixture should have a thick, gloopy consistency, like creamy polenta. Remove it from the heat and let it cool a bit.

*   *   *

Whisk together the cream and eggs and add them to the pumpkin mixture. Pour the mixture into the cooled pie crust, and bake for 40 to 50 minutes, until the sides are set and you still have a quarter-sized wiggly puddle in the center. Remove the pie from the oven and cool it on a wire rack. The pie will finish baking as it cools. The pie should be completely cool before serving. Enjoy.

Deanna Smith **Des Moines, Iowa**

Deanna was sixteen when she made her first pie for her boyfriend, who is now her husband of forty years. It was a pecan pie, and she followed a recipe from a cookbook. She started entering pie contests at the Iowa State Fair three years ago and has won eight ribbons for her efforts. She enjoys entering baking contests with her sister, Anita, whose peach pie placed second behind hers at the fair this year. She says the two of them seem to alternate winning contests, so everything evens out.

Deanna's Pie Contest Tips: "You can buy small leaf and fruit cookie cutters to decorate pies. You can also come up with your own style of crimping the crust. Just be creative and enjoy pie baking. I use a glass pie plate because I think it makes the best pies, and the judges can see the evenly browned bottom of the crust. Also, you have to realize that judges have their own tastes. A judge once said my chocolate pie was the best chocolate thing she'd ever put in her mouth, while another gave it third place, so you never know. You just have to bake the very best pie you know how to make."

FRESH PEACH PIE
by Deanna Smith

First-Prize Winner at the 2010 Iowa State Fair "Oh My! It's Peach Pie!" Competition

CRUST

* 1½ cups all-purpose flour
* ½ cup cake flour
* ½ tablespoon sugar
* ½ teaspoon salt
* ½ cup Butter Flavor Crisco, chilled
* 3 tablespoons unsalted butter, very cold
* 5 to 7 tablespoons ice water mixture (recipe follows)

ICE WATER MIXTURE
* 1 cup cold water
* 1 tablespoon apple cider vinegar
* 1 egg, beaten

Combine ingredients in a 2-cup measuring cup. Fill the rest of the cup with ice.

FILLING

* 8 to 9 medium peaches, peeled, pitted, and sliced to ⅓ inch thick (I use a serrated blade peeler)
* 1 cup plus 2 teaspoons sugar
* 1 tablespoon cornstarch
* 1 tablespoon fresh lemon juice
* ¼ teaspoon cinnamon
* ⅛ teaspoon fresh grated nutmeg
* ¼ teaspoon real almond extract
* ⅛ teaspoon salt
* 2 teaspoons sugar

Before beginning the crust, place the peach slices and sugar for the filling in a large bowl for one hour.

* * *

To make the crust, whisk the flours, sugar, and salt till combined. Cut in the Crisco until the mixture resembles coarse crumbs about the size of small peas. Cut in the butter, leaving some pieces a little larger. Add ice water mixture 1 tablespoon at a time while tossing with a fork. When you add the last tablespoon of ice water mixture, toss the dough with your fingertips and then divide it into 2 balls and flatten each into a disc. Wrap the discs in plastic wrap or place in freezer bag. Set the discs in the fridge to rest for at least an hour. At this point, dough can be refrigerated for up to 2 days or frozen for up to 2 months.

* * *

After the dough has rested, lightly dust a clean work surface with flour. To make the lattice crust, roll one of the discs into a 10 by 12-inch rectangle. Use a crimped pastry cutter to cut the dough into 1¼ by 12-inch strips and place them in a 9-inch glass pie pan. Cover the strips with plastic wrap and chill the dough for another 30 minutes to an hour, as this makes the strips a lot easier to work with.

* * *

While the strips rest in the refrigerator, drain the peaches thoroughly: Put them into a colander placed in a bowl to reserve the juice. Let drain for an

hour, stirring 2 or 3 times to get the juice out, and then pour the juice into a small saucepan and set aside.

❄ ❄ ❄

Roll the other dough disc into a 12-inch circle on a lightly floured work surface, then gently place it in a 9-inch pie plate, letting an inch of the excess dough hang over the edge, trimming where necessary.

❄ ❄ ❄

Preheat the oven to 400°F. Place a sheet pan on the bottom rack.

❄ ❄ ❄

To make the filling, bring the peach juice to a boil, decrease the heat, and simmer for 12 to 15 minutes, until the juice is reduced to ½ cup, swirling the pan occasionally.

❄ ❄ ❄

In a large bowl, dissolve the cornstarch in the lemon juice and then toss the drained peaches, the reduced juice (reserving 1 tablespoon), cinnamon, nutmeg, almond extract, and salt together until well combined. Spread the fruit mixture into the dough-lined pie plate.

❄ ❄ ❄

Lay four parallel strips evenly over the filling. Starting just to the side of the middle of the opposite direction, weave a fifth strip. Continue to weave in the remaining three strips. Cut the strips even with the edge of the pie plate. Fold the excess inch of bottom crust dough inward over the lattice and crimp it evenly around the edges.

* * *

Sprinkle the top of the pie with sugar and place it on the heated baking sheet. Bake for 25 minutes. Reduce the oven temperature to 365°F. Move the pie to the center rack and bake for 25 to 30 minutes more. If the crust is browning too fast, cover it with aluminum foil or a pie ring. Remove the pie from the oven and brush the top with the reserved reduced juice. Let the pie cool on a wire rack for 2 hours.

Barbara Treves **Los Angeles, California**

Originally from Toronto, Canada, Barbara learned the basics of baking from her mother when she was a child. She took her lessons and ran with them, often coming home from school and whipping together cakes, cookies, and fudge. She didn't attempt pies until her twenties, when she started experimenting with different recipes. She's called Los Angeles her home for more than twenty-five years now; it's where she works as an interior designer and lives with her husband and teenage son. Her apple and pumpkin pies, in particular, are always requested for family holiday dinners. She entered the pie contest on a whim, having been laid off from work and wanting to do something fun and different from anything she had ever done. Barbara says that winning not just Best in Category, but Best in Show as well, was a thrill of a lifetime for her.

Barbara's Pie Contest Tips: "Test out your recipe in advance by having a few close friends and/or family members do the taste test and then give you their opinions. Consider them and tweak the recipe as you see fit. Also, always use the freshest and purest ingredients, give yourself plenty of time, stay relaxed, and have fun!"

BLUE RIBBON PIE RECIPES AND TIPS FROM THE CHAMPION BAKERS

FOREVER FAVORITE APPLE PIE

by Barbara Treves

Best in Show Winner at KCRW's 2009 Good Food Pie Contest

CRUST

* 1½ cups organic whole wheat pastry flour
* 1 cup organic unbleached, all-purpose flour
* 2 teaspoons salt
* 1 tablespoon vanilla powder
* 1 vanilla bean, split, seeds scraped
* 3 tablespoons organic sugar
* 1¼ cup unsalted sweet butter (freshly made if possible), chilled and diced
* 1 tablespoon white vinegar, chilled
* 6 to 8 tablespoons ice water

FILLING

* ½ cup dried sour cherries
* ¼ cup Calvados apple brandy
* 4 tablespoons organic unbleached, all-purpose flour
* 1 vanilla bean, split, seeds scraped
* 12 organic apples from local farmers market (mixture of Granny Smith, Fuji, or other tart, crisp apples taste the best), peeled, cored, and sliced.
* 1½ teaspoons ground cinnamon
* ¼ teaspoon ground nutmeg
* ¼ teaspoon ground cloves
* 1 cup organic sugar
* 1 teaspoon salt

* 2 teaspoons vanilla extract
* ¼ cup apple cider vinegar
* 4 tablespoons unsalted sweet butter (freshly made if possible)
* 1 tablespoon heavy cream

FINAL TOPPING

* 1 egg
* 1 tablespoon heavy cream
* 1 to 2 tablespoons of turbinado raw sugar

43

Before beginning the crust, soak the cherries in the brandy for the filling for at least 2 hours.

✳ ✳ ✳

To make the crust, combine the flours, salt, vanilla powder, vanilla bean, and sugar and place the mixture in the freezer. Chill butter and vinegar in the refrigerator for at least 1 hour prior to preparation.

✳ ✳ ✳

When ready, in the work bowl of a food processor fitted with a metal blade, pulse the flour mixture to mix thoroughly. Add the butter and pulse a few times to cut the fat into the flour. The mixture should resemble pea-sized meal. Add the vinegar, pulse to mix, and then add the ice water, 1 tablespoon at a time, until the dough begins to stick together and when pinched by hand, holds together. Stop the machine. Lay a piece of wax paper on the counter and dump the dough onto it, scraping the bowl and blade with a spatula. Pat the dough into a ball, wrap lightly, and chill—along with a 9-inch pie plate—for at least an hour before using. At this point, dough can be refrigerated for up to 2 days or frozen for up to 2 months.

✳ ✳ ✳

While the dough chills, make the filling. Preheat broiler. Toss the sliced apples, vanilla bean seed, cinnamon, nutmeg, cloves, and 2 tablespoons of the sugar together and place in a roasting pan. Broil until the apples are slightly browned but not cooked through. Once the apples are nicely browned and caramelized, transfer the apples to a bowl and add the cherry mixture, remaining sugar, four, salt, vanilla extract, vinegar, and cream. Stir to combine.

❄ ❄ ❄

After the dough has rested, preheat the oven to 400°F. Lightly dust a clean work surface with flour, and roll out the first disc of dough to a circle approximately 10 inches in diameter and about ⅛ inch thick. Line your chilled pie plate with the dough and trim the overhang to about ½ inch. Tuck the overhang under the edge between the pie plate and the crust.

❄ ❄ ❄

Add the broiled apples mixture, then dot with the butter. Roll out your second disc of dough into a circle about ⅛ inch thick and place it on top of the apples. Pinch the top and bottom of the dough edges together to form a decorative edge and vent the top.

❄ ❄ ❄

For the final topping, beat the egg and cream together in a small dish then brush the mixture on the top and edges of the pie. Sprinkle with sugar.

❄ ❄ ❄

Bake for 45 minutes. If the crust is browning too fast, cover it with aluminum foil or a pie ring. Turn the pie in the oven and cook it an additional 15 minutes or until done. Remove the pie from the oven and cool it on a wire rack for at least 2 hours prior to serving.

Dorothy O. Naylor
Calais, Vermont

Dorothy grew up in Southampton, Massachusetts, where she learned to cook from her mother, Dorothy Harvest Openshaw, whose family emigrated from England. The cooking style was quite plain, incorporating few herbs or spices. Looking back, Dorothy thinks she made the things her family loved so often that practice simply made perfect. A retired teacher, she has lived with her family in Calais, Vermont, for the past forty-three years. She won the pie contest using her mother's apple pie filling recipe.

Dorothy's Pie Contest Tip: "Use your basic recipe that you (and others) love—don't try tweaking it. Just use the best ingredients in the usual way."

APPLE PIE

by Dorothy O. Naylor

**First-Prize Winner at the 2009 Hancock Shaker Village
Country Fair Pie Contest in Pittsfield, Massachusetts**

CRUST

Dorothy made the Cooks Illustrated *recipe for
Foolproof Pie Dough, which uses vodka as the
key ingredient to help keep the crust moist. (See*
Cooks Illustrated, *November 2007, or search
online for the recipe.)*

FILLING

* 6 apples—3 or 4 Granny Smith (for
  firm texture) and 2 or 3 McIntosh
  (for flavor)

* 5 or 6 whole cloves

* 1⅓ cups sugar

* 1 heaping teaspoon cinnamon

* Half and half or light cream, for
  washing crust prior to baking

Lightly dust a clean work surface with flour, and roll out the first disc of dough to a circle approximately 10 inches in diameter and about ⅛ inch thick. Line your pie plate with the dough and trim the overhang to about ½ inch. Tuck the overhang under the edge between the pie plate and the crust.

❋ ❋ ❋

Preheat the oven to 400°F. Peel, core, and slice the apples——make sure you have enough to mound up slightly in your pie plate, which should not be shallow. I slice out the core (from bottom to top works best) and slice up the rest, making 4 or 5 slices per quarter depending on the size of the apple.

❋ ❋ ❋

Scatter the cloves among the apples in the pie plate. Shake up the sugar and cinnamon in a jar so they are well mixed, then sprinkle it over the apples.

❋ ❋ ❋

Place the top crust on and seal it to the bottom crust in the usual manner.

❋ ❋ ❋

Wash the crust with half and half. Make slits in the crust to release steam.

❋ ❋ ❋

Cook for about 20 minutes. Reduce the oven temperature to 350°F and cook for 25 more minutes. If the crust is browning too fast, cover it with aluminum foil or a pie ring. Remove the pie from the oven and let cool on a wire rack.

Susan Asato **Aliso Viejo, California**

Susan was born and raised in Hawaii and now lives in Orange County, California, with her human love, Ryan, and rescued mixed-breed dog, Grommit. She has a degree in applied mathematics and is an engineer by trade. Her motivation for entering recipe contests is to help show that vegan food can hold its own alongside nonvegan food. "We do not have to give up decadent foods in order to live more consciously and compassionately," she says. "I think people are more likely to believe this when they hear that vegan food wins awards over nonvegan food in competitive settings."

Susan's Pie Contest Tips: "Vegan food contains no animal or animal-based ingredients — no butter, lard, eggs, milk, cream, gelatin, cheese, or honey. Many people ask how I get my crusts so flaky and 'buttery' without butter. Luckily, there is a simple vegan butter substitute called Earth Balance. It doesn't contain any hydrogenated oils, is non-GMO, tastes just as rich and creamy as butter, and acts like it in baking. There are less-expensive butter substitutes available; however, a high-quality product such as Earth Balance can easily taste and perform better than some low-quality dairy butters."

BLUE RIBBON PIE RECIPES AND TIPS FROM THE CHAMPION BAKERS

VEGAN APPLE PIE with CRUNCHY PECAN TOPPING and LIME GLAZE

by Susan Asato

First-Prize Winner at the 2009 Orange County Fair in California

CRUST

* ½ cup (1 stick) nondairy, nonhydrogenated vegan butter, chilled and diced
* 3 tablespoons nonhydrogenated vegan vegetable shortening, chilled and diced
* 1⅔ cups unbleached all-purpose flour
* 1 tablespoon sugar (non-bone-char processed)
* ¼ teaspoon salt
* 2 to 4 tablespoons ice water

APPLE FILLING

* 4 to 6 Granny Smith apples, medium
* 4 to 6 Fuji apples, medium
* ⅓ cup lime juice, freshly squeezed (about 3 limes)
* ⅓ cup sugar (non-bone-char processed)
* 2 tablespoons agave nectar
* 4 tablespoons tapioca flour
* 2 tablespoons unbleached all-purpose flour
* 1 teaspoon cinnamon
* ¼ teaspoon salt

CRUMB TOPPING

* ⅓ cup nondairy, nonhydrogenated vegan butter

* ½ cup pecans, chopped and toasted

* ⅔ cup firmly packed light brown sugar (non-bone-char processed)

* ½ cup flour

* ½ cup multigrain dry hot cereal mix (rolled grains)

* ¾ teaspoon cinnamon

* ¼ teaspoon nutmeg

GLAZE

* ½ cup powdered sugar (non-bone-char processed)

* 1 to 2 tablespoons lime juice, freshly squeezed (about 1 lime)

* ⅛ teaspoon vanilla extract

* Pinch of salt

✳ ✳ ✳

To make the crust, in the work bowl of a food processor, pulse the butter, shortening, flour, sugar, and salt until ingredients are incorporated. Add 2 to 4 tablespoons of ice water (amount will vary depending on kitchen temperature and humidity) and pulse until the mixture holds its shape when a small amount is squeezed in your fist. Lay a piece of plastic wrap on the counter and dump the dough onto it, scraping the bowl and blade with a spatula. Pat the dough into a ball, wrap lightly, and chill for at least an hour before using. At this point, dough can be refrigerated for up to 2 days or frozen for up to 2 months.

✳ ✳ ✳

After the dough has rested, preheat the oven to 375°F and lightly dust a clean work surface with flour. Roll out the dough to a circle approximately 10 inches in diameter and about ⅛ inch thick. Line a 9-inch lightly greased deep-dish pie pan with the dough; crimp the edges and dock the bottom. Bake for 14 to 15 minutes, until crust is very lightly browned, then allow to cool for at least 30 minutes.

✳ ✳ ✳

While the crust cools, peel and thinly slice the apples (about ⅛ inch thick) and place them in a large bowl. Gradually add ⅓ cup of lime juice to moisten the apples while prepping to prevent browning. Add the sugar, agave nectar, flours, cinnamon, and salt and gently mix together well.

In a separate bowl, mix together all crumb topping ingredients well using a fork.

※ ※ ※

Fill the cooled pie crust with the apple mixture using a slotted spoon and your hands. Spoon the crumb topping evenly over the apples.

※ ※ ※

Place the pie on a sheet pan and bake for 25 to 30 minutes. When the topping and crust edges are lightly browned, loosely cover the entire pie with aluminum foil, reduce the temperature to 350°F, and bake for an additional 35 to 40 minutes. Remove the pie from the oven and let cool on a wire rack for at least 2 hours.

※ ※ ※

For the glaze, sift powdered sugar into a small bowl. Add 1 tablespoon of the lime juice and mix well. Gradually add additional lime juice, several drops at a time, until it reaches the consistency of maple syrup or a little thicker for a more opaque appearance. Add vanilla extract and salt. Pipe the glaze in a lattice pattern onto the cooled pie.

Jane Robbins Nashville, Tennessee

Jane is a management professor who summers in Little Compton, Rhode Island, and writes a blog on the food of Rhode Island and New England called "Little Compton Mornings" (www.little comptonmornings. blogspot.com). She learned to cook and

bake by watching her Pennsylvania Dutch grandmother and by eating good homemade food. She adores pie, particularly fruit pies, and particularly for breakfast. She deems the combination of fruit, sugar, spice, and pastry to be "pure genius."

Jane's Pie Contest Tips: "Use the best possible ingredients; time the making of your pie so that it is freshly made the day of the contest but allowed to cool to proper eating temperature before judging; do not refrigerate your pie unless it is designed to be eaten cold. Also, use lard in your crust for all fruit pies; don't over-spice, over-thicken, or over-sweeten."

GRANDMA'S BROWN SUGAR PIE
by Jane Robbins

**First-Prize Winner at the 2006 Tiverton Land Trust
"Country Day at Pardon Gray" Pie Contest in Rhode Island**

My grandmother was Pennsylvania Dutch and was an expert baker of all sorts of pies and cakes. This is my standard lard/butter crust recipe, and the way she made the filling. The pie has a creamy, not firm, texture.

CRUST
* ❋ 3 tablespoons unsalted butter, chilled
* ❋ 3 tablespoons lard, chilled
* ❋ 1⅓ cups all-purpose flour
* ❋ ⅓ teaspoon salt
* ❋ 2 to 4 tablespoons ice water

FILLING
* ❋ 1 cup firmly packed brown sugar
* ❋ 3 tablespoons all-purpose flour
* ❋ Pinch of salt
* ❋ 1 (12-ounce) can evaporated milk, or 1½ cups light cream
* ❋ 3 tablespoons unsalted butter
* ❋ Ground cinnamon or 3:1 mixture of ground cinnamon and nutmeg

Cut the butter and lard into the flour and salt rapidly with your fingers or using two sharp knives. Gradually add the water, blending with a fork, until the dough just comes together; the amount of water will depend on the weather, so start with the smaller amount. Turn the dough onto a board and, with the palm of your hand, smear from the center outward; do not overwork. Form the dough into a disc, wrap it in wax paper, and chill for at least an hour. You can also make it in a food processer. Pulse the flour and salt, just to combine. Add the butter and lard, and pulse a few times to cut the fat into the flour. Add the water gradually through the feed tube while the machine is running until the pastry forms a ball, at which point it is ready to be chilled.

✳ ✳ ✳

After the dough has rested, lightly dust a clean work surface with flour, and roll out to a circle approximately 10 to 11 inches in diameter and about ⅛ inch thick. Line an 8-inch pie plate with the dough, turn the overhang under to sit on the rim of the plate, and flute the edge. Return the crust to the fridge to chill for another 20 to 30 minutes.

✳ ✳ ✳

Preheat the oven to 350°F and place rack in middle position. Place the brown sugar, flour, and salt into the chilled unbaked pie shell and, using your hands, lightly combine and distribute it evenly, being careful not to scratch the pastry. Pour the milk over all; do not stir. Dot with the butter, and sift cinnamon (or a mixture of 3 parts cinnamon and 1 part nutmeg) across the entire surface of the pie to cover. Bake for about 50 minutes, until the filling bubbles gently; the pie will set but be quivery. Remove the pie from the oven and let it cool on a wire rack. Serve at room temperature, plain or with unsweetened whipped cream.

Karla Noble Pie Town, New Mexico

Karla and her husband, both retired, are full-time RVers who divide their time among Mexico, traveling, and Pie Town, New Mexico. She credits her grandmother with initially teaching her baking skills, but she also learned many tips from various bakers during her career in food service management. She loves pie because there are so many ways to change the dough and filling.

Karla's Pie Contest Tips: "I think the difference between a good and great pie is visual. The first rule of food service is: You eat with your eyes first. Taste is certainly important as well, but if it doesn't look great, you probably won't think it tastes exceptional, either. Don't be afraid to enter the contest. Allow plenty of time for preparing the pie, and stay relaxed."

PINEAPPLE PIE with COCONUT MACADAMIA NUT TOPPING

by Karla Noble

First-Place Winner—Fruit Category at the 2009 Pie Town
Pie Festival Pie-Baking Contest

FILLING
* ½ cup sugar
* 3 tablespoons cornstarch
* ¼ teaspoon salt
* 2 (20-ounce) cans crushed pineapple in juice, undrained (about 4 cups)

CRUST
* 1 cup all-purpose flour
* ½ teaspoon salt
* ⅓ cup shortening
* 3 to 4 tablespoons ice water

CRUMB TOPPING
* 1 (9-ounce) package Jiffy Golden Yellow Cake Mix
* ¼ cup unsalted butter, softened
* ⅔ cup sweetened coconut
* 1 (2.34-ounce) package macadamia nuts

First, make the filling. In a small bowl, combine the sugar, cornstarch, and salt. Pour the pineapple with juice into a saucepan, add the sugar mixture, and stir to combine. Cook over medium heat, stirring constantly, for 10 to 12 minutes, until thickened. Cool slightly while preparing the pie dough.

* * *

Preheat the oven to 375°F and place the oven rack in the middle position.

* * *

In a mixing bowl, combine the flour and salt. Cut in the shortening using a pastry blender, until the coarse mixture resembles small peas. Sprinkle water over the mixture 1 tablespoon at a time while stirring with a fork. Add water until the dough is just moist enough to hold together. Turn the dough onto a board and, with the palm of your hand, smear from the center outward; do not overwork. Form the dough into a disc, about ½ inch thick, and roll it out to a circle approximately 10 inches in diameter and about ⅛ inch thick. Fold pastry in half and transfer to a 9-inch pie pan. Unfold and fit the dough loosely into the pan, gently patting out any air pockets. Fold the extra inch of dough under and flute the edge around the pan.

* * *

For the crumb topping, pour the dry cake mix into a small mixing bowl. Add the softened butter and stir to combine. In a food processor or blender, chop the coconut and nuts together until the nuts are diced and medium-sized. Add the coconut mixture to the cake mixture. Toss with a fork until well blended and crumbly.

❊ ❊ ❊

Pour the slightly cooled pineapple mixture into the prepared crust. Sprinkle crumb topping on top of the pie until well covered. (You may not need all the topping.)

❊ ❊ ❊

Place pie on the middle oven rack and bake for about 40 minutes, or until the crust and topping are golden brown. Remove the pie from the oven and let it cool on a wire rack for at least 2 hours before serving. I think the flavors of the pie are better served slightly warm, so I would suggest serving when the bottom of the pie plate is warm to the touch, but not hot.

Kate Stewart Rovner **Plano, Texas**

Kate had won first, second, and third place ribbons at the State Fair of Texas, but the American Pie Council Crisco National Pie Championships was the first time she ever won Best of Show. A stay-at-home mom, she comes from a long line of great pie bakers. Both of her grandmothers made pies—her Grandma Hazel made lemon meringue and her Grandma Lucy made cherry pie. She also has aunts who are wonderful pie bakers, and her mother is a great pie baker, too. Kate says, "I guess that's why I love pie—it reminds me of the wonderful women of my family."

Kate's Pie Contest Tip: "I make pies that my family likes to eat, not pies just to win competitions. That way, even if I don't win, my family is very happy!"

LEMON SWIRL CREAM CHEESE PIE

by Kate Stewart Rovner

**Best of Show Winner at the 2010 American Pie Council
Crisco National Pie Championships**

LEMON CURD

* 1 teaspoon finely grated lemon zest
* ½ cup fresh lemon juice
* ½ cup sugar
* 3 eggs, lightly beaten
* ¼ cup unsalted butter, cut into small cubes

VANILLA WAFER CRUMB CRUST

* 1½ cups vanilla wafer crumbs
* ¾ cup almonds, toasted and finely ground
* 2 teaspoons lemon zest
* Pinch of salt
* 7 tablespoons melted butter

LEMON CREAM CHEESE FILLING

* 2 (8-ounce) packages Philadelphia brand cream cheese, softened
* ⅔ cup sugar
* 2 eggs
* ½ cup sour cream
* ½ teaspoon vanilla
* ⅓ teaspoon lemon extract
* Reserved lemon curd

GARNISH

* ½ cup heavy whipping cream
* 2 tablespoons powdered sugar
* ½ teaspoon vanilla
* 12 to 15 fresh raspberries
* 1 lemon, cut into thin slices and quartered

63

First, prepare the lemon curd. In a 1½-quart saucepan, whisk together the lemon zest, lemon juice, and sugar. Whisk in the eggs and butter. Cook over medium-low heat, whisking frequently for 7 minutes, or until curd is thick. Remove from the heat and use a food mill or sieve to strain the curd into a small bowl. Remove ½ cup of the lemon curd, reserving the rest. Press plastic wrap directly onto the surfaces. Cool 30 minutes.

* * *

Preheat the oven to 350°F and place the rack on the bottom level. Spray a 9-inch pie plate with Crisco No-Stick spray and prepare the vanilla wafer crumb crust.

* * *

In a medium mixing bowl, use a fork to toss together the vanilla wafer crumbs, almonds, lemon zest, and salt. Stir in the melted butter. Press the mixture onto the bottom and sides of a prepared pie plate.

* * *

Bake for 12 minutes on the bottom oven rack. Remove from the oven and set aside.

* * *

For the cream cheese filling, beat the cream cheese and sugar at medium speed in a medium mixing bowl for 2 minutes, or until smooth. Add the eggs, one at a time, and beat at low speed until incorporated. Beat in the sour cream, vanilla, and lemon extract. Beat in the reserved lemon curd. Pour the mixture

into the baked crust. Dollop the remaining ½ cup of lemon curd onto the filling and swirl with a small knife.

* * *

Bake for 30 minutes, or until the center is nearly set. Remove from the oven and cool on a wire rack for 2 hours. Cover and refrigerate overnight.

* * *

For the garnish, in a chilled medium mixing bowl, beat the whipping cream, powdered sugar, and vanilla with a handheld electric mixer, starting at the lowest speed and increasing gradually each minute, until stiff peaks are formed. Using a number 32 tip, pipe whipped cream decoratively around the border of the pie. Decorate with fresh raspberries and lemon slices. Refrigerate until serving time.

Adam Janowski **Bonita Springs, Florida**

Adam is a school library media special-
ist who learned to cook from his Polish
American family in Detroit, Michigan. He
writes about his family's recipes on his
blog "From My Family's Kitchen" (www.
apolishkitchen.blogspot.com). Adam finds
that baking soothes him in times of stress.
The first time he bakes something, he
always follows the recipe exactly. He then
analyzes the results and makes changes as
needed before making it again.

Adam's Pie Contest Tips: "I have two tips for entering a pie-baking contest. First, presentation is really important. You only get a brief chance for the judges to look at your pie and
compare it with the other pies. Be sure it looks great. I tend to put more filling in a contest
pie than I would for a pie I make for friends or family. My second tip is chocolate, chocolate,
and chocolate. It seems to be the favorite of judges. When I make a pastry crust, I add a
half teaspoon of white vinegar to the ice water that will be added to the flour and shortening
mixture. It makes for a very tender crust that is easy to roll out."

BLACK-BOTTOM PEANUT BUTTER MOUSSE PIE

by Adam Janowski

Grand Prize Winner at the 2010 Zonta Club of Bonita Springs
Best Blue Ribbon Pie Contest

CRUST

* 20 Oreo cookies
* ¼ cup butter, melted

GANACHE

* 1⅓ cups semisweet chocolate chips (about 8 ounces)
* ⅔ cup whipping cream
* 2 tablespoons light corn syrup
* 1 teaspoon vanilla extract

MOUSSE

* 1 teaspoon unflavored gelatin
* 1 tablespoon cold water
* 3 tablespoons milk
* 1 cup smooth peanut butter
* ½ cup powdered sugar
* 1 teaspoon vanilla extract
* 1¾ cups whipping cream, divided

GARNISH

* ¼ cup reserved chocolate ganache
* 1 cup whipping cream
* 3 tablespoons powdered sugar
* ½ cup honey roasted peanuts
* 6 mini Reese's Peanut Butter Cups, halved

Preheat the oven to 350°F. Place the Oreos in a food processor or blender and process until finely crumbled. Empty the crumbs into a mixing bowl and stir in the melted butter until well combined. Pat wet crumbs all over and up the sides of a 10-inch pie pan, making an even surface. Bake the crust for 8 to 10 minutes, until hardened. Cool before filling.

✳ ✳ ✳

For the ganache, in the top of a double boiler, combine the chocolate chips, whipping cream, corn syrup, and vanilla. Whisk until melted and smooth. Spread the chocolate mixture over the bottom of the crust, reserving ¼ cup for the garnish. Refrigerate until cool, and prepare the mousse.

✳ ✳ ✳

Dissolve the gelatin in the cold water. Let sit for about 5 minutes. In a small saucepan, heat the milk to almost boiling, then remove from heat. Add the gelatin to the milk and whisk until gelatin is completely dissolved. Allow to come to room temperature. Meanwhile, in a large bowl, combine the peanut butter, powdered sugar, vanilla, and ¾ cup of the whipping cream. Whisk until smooth. In a medium bowl, beat the remaining 1 cup of cream until soft peaks form. While still beating, pour in the milk mixture. Continue beating until stiff peaks form. Fold into the peanut butter mixture in 3 parts. Spread the mousse over the chocolate layer. Chill at least 1 hour.

✳ ✳ ✳

For the garnish, drizzle the reserved ganache over the peanut butter mousse layer in a crisscross pattern. (You may need to whisk in a little whipping cream to make it spreadable.) Whip cream until soft peaks form. Add powdered sugar and continue whipping until peaks are stiff. Do not overbeat. Pipe whipping cream around the edge of the pie. Garnish with honey roasted peanuts (chopped if desired). Tuck peanut butter cup halves into the whipping cream around the edge of the pie. Chill at least 3 hours before serving.

Alison Greco **Portland, Oregon**

Alison's family hails from Arkansas. Her great-grandmother Mama Moore taught her to bake traditional southern pies in her little trailer. "She made a stunning chocolate cream pie with meringue topping that I dreamed about between trips to see her," says Alison. Now, Alison holds a doctorate in clinical psychology and runs a user experience group for a company that makes software for child care and education centers. She finds cooking to be a creative outlet, as well as a way to nourish (and treat) her family. The Portland Pie-Off was her first cooking contest ever and she was astonished when she won.

Alison's Pie Contest Tips: "For pie contests, or really any competition, know your audience. The Portland Pie-Off rewards creativity and unusual flavor combinations, so I knew my pie would have a good chance. But if I were entering the Oregon State Fair, I would have been more conservative and spent more time and attention on execution and presentation."

CUCUMBER HONEYDEW WHITE CHOCOLATE PUDDING ICEBOX PIE

by Alison Greco

Grand Prize Winner of the 2009 Portland Pie-Off

SORBET

* 2 cups peeled, seeded, and cubed honeydew melon
* 1 cup peeled, seeded, and cubed cucumber
* ¾ cup sugar
* 2 tablespoons light corn syrup
* 3 tablespoons lime juice

CRUST

* 2½ cups crushed shortbread cookies
* 6 tablespoons butter, melted

WHITE CHOCOLATE PUDDING

* 2½ cups whole milk
* Pinch of salt
* ½ cup sugar
* 3 tablespoons cornstarch
* 2 egg yolks
* 1 teaspoon vanilla extract
* 1 tablespoon unsalted butter
* 1 cup white chocolate chips

71

To make the sorbet, in a blender or food processor that has been fitted with a metal blade, combine the honeydew, cucumber, sugar, corn syrup, and lime juice. Pulse to chop, then process until thick and smooth. Place mixture in an ice cream maker and freeze according to manufacturer's instructions. Place in the freezer to ripen while you make the crust and pudding.

❄ ❄ ❄

For the crust, preheat the oven to 375°F. In a small bowl, combine the shortbread crumbs and butter and blend well. Press into the bottom and up the sides of a 9-inch pie plate. Bake for 10 to 12 minutes, until crust is lightly browned. Cool on a wire rack before filling.

❄ ❄ ❄

To make the pudding, place 2 cups of the milk and the salt in a medium, heavy-bottomed saucepan. Sprinkle the sugar on the milk but do not stir; cook over medium-high heat. While the milk mixture is heating, in a small bowl, quickly combine the cornstarch with the remaining ½ cup of milk; add egg yolks and mix well. When the milk mixture comes to a full boil, remove the saucepan from the heat and stir in the cornstarch mixture. The pudding will begin to thicken. Return the mixture to the heat and cook, stirring continuously, for 1 minute. Remove from the heat, and stir in the vanilla, butter, and chocolate chips. Place plastic wrap on the surface and chill in the refrigerator until cool.

❄ ❄ ❄

To assemble the pie, take the sorbet out of the freezer and allow it to soften so it can easily be spread. Spread 2 cups of the chilled pudding in the crust (you may need to strain the pudding through a wire mesh strainer if lumps have formed). The recipe may make more than 2 cups of pudding. You can save the remainder and serve as a separate dessert (so good with piroulines!). Place the pie in the freezer until the pudding hardens, about 20 minutes. Remove the pie from the freezer and spread the softened sorbet over the pudding. Return to the freezer to harden. Thaw pie for a few minutes before serving so it gets soft enough to cut, or heat a knife under very hot water to cleanly cut slices.

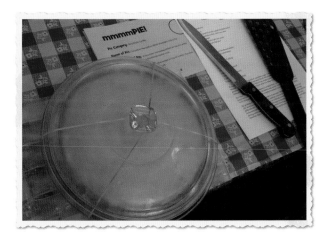

Andy McCrary
Smithville, Georgia

Andy is an electrician and rancher. His late wife taught him how to make chicken pie, and this recipe is an old one from her family. It has garnered five first-place ribbons for his family. He assisted his daughter in winning two pie festivals, and he has won

three personally. He says he loves pie because it is comfort food and delicious.

Andy's Pie Contest Tips: "Do not be discouraged if at first you do not win. The first time we entered we did not place, the second time we won second place, and after that first place each time. Note and observe the other contestants who enter. Make your pie as attractive as possible. We wrote a poem one year to go with our entry that reflected the beginnings and history of the festival. Accessories can make your entry more appealing. We have used flowers, fruit, figurines, and a handmade serving board. I prefer baking in a gas oven."

CHICKEN PIE
by *Andy McCrary*

First-Prize Winner at the 2009 Smithville Chicken Pie Contest

Chicken pie does not have vegetables; chicken pot pie does. We did not enter a chicken pot pie festival—ours is a chicken pie festival.

* 1 chicken
* 3 hard-boiled eggs, peeled and sliced thinly
* 1¾ cups of chicken broth
* 1 can cream of chicken soup
* Salt and pepper
* 1 cup self-rising flour
* 1 stick of margarine or butter, melted

* 1 cup milk
* 1 package of pie crust dough from the dairy section of the grocery store

Smithville Chicken Pie Contest photos by Betsy Usry

75

Boil one chicken until thoroughly cooked and tender. Debone and slice meat into chunky pieces.

* * *

Preheat the oven to 350°F. Spray a 9 by 13-inch Pyrex pan with nonstick spray. Place the sliced chicken in the pan. Layer the sliced eggs over the chicken evenly.

* * *

In a medium bowl, mix 1½ cups of the chicken broth and the soup. Stir until smooth, and pour over the chicken and eggs. Season as desired with salt and pepper. In another medium bowl, mix the flour, the remaining ¼ cup of chicken broth, the margarine, and the milk until smooth, and pour over the chicken and eggs. This will make the basic crust.

* * *

For the sake of appearance for competition, we used a lattice-work crust and put it on for the last 20 minutes of baking. The additional crust is not necessary, but makes a pretty product if you are in a contest. Just buy a package of pie crust from the dairy case, cut it into strips with a pizza wheel, weave the lattice to fit the pan, freeze the whole thing on a cookie sheet, and when firm, transfer to the dish with the pie and brush with milk to make it brown pretty. And that's it!

* * *

Bake for 55 minutes, then add lattice crust and bake for another 20 minutes, until the crust is golden brown.

❊ ❊ ❊

Here in South Georgia we serve this pie with black-eyed peas, cornbread, fried fatback, and sweet tea. Now, sit back and enjoy.

Here is the poem that Andy's wife, Kathy H. W. McCrary, wrote about chicken pie in 2006.

Chicken Pie, Oh My

In a little town in Southwest Georgia, at the turn of the century,
Hungry train passengers made a discovery that was plain.
The place to go, the place to know for chicken pie was
Smithville, Georgia.
The McAfee Hotel, or so the old timers tell,
Just always fit the bill.
A tradition began then and continues to this day.
When it comes to chicken pie, the Smithville folks just don't play.

Queen Esther New York, New York

Singer and actress Queen Esther grew up in Charleston, South Carolina, with a large, loving extended family that included grandparents and great-grandparents. She says her mother made the best sweet potato pies—that she was an effortless baker who used very simple ingredients and never measured anything. For Queen Esther, baking pie is a way to keep her creative juices flowing. "It's a lovely way to get lost in my own home," she says. "When I bake, something clicks and I stop thinking—and that's when real creativity tends to emerge."

Photo by Josh Lowenthal

Queen Esther's Pie Contest Tip: "Only one—be yourself. Make it up as you go along, and more of you will be in what you create than you'd dare to think."

SWEET APPLEWOOD-SMOKED BACON APPLE PIE

by Queen Esther

Best Savory Pie Winner at the 2010 Roaring '20s Jazz Age
Lawn Party Pie Contest on New York's Governors Island

CRUST

* ⅔ cup shortening

* 2 cups all-purpose flour

* 1 to 3 tablespoons cold water,
  or a bit more as needed

FILLING

* 8 to 10 medium/large Granny Smith
  apples

* 7 slices of applewood-smoked bacon

* 4 tablespoons of unsalted butter,
  sliced

* ½ lemon

* 3 tablespoons clover honey

* ¼ cup all-purpose flour

* ¼ cup firmly packed brown sugar

* ½ teaspoon ginger

* ½ teaspoon allspice

* 1 tablespoon cinnamon

* ½ teaspoon ground cloves

Preheat the oven to 400°F. While you peel and thinly slice the apples, cook the bacon slowly until it's soft and chewy—not hard. Dice the butter by taking a pat and cutting into fourths. Set sliced apples, bacon, and butter aside, while you prepare the crust.

❄ ❄ ❄

Mix the shortening and flour together gradually with a fork and add water until the dough reaches the appropriate consistency. Cut the dough in half and roll out onto a floured surface with a rolling pin, placing one round section into a 9-inch pie pan, cutting the edges where appropriate. Roll out and shape the top and set aside.

❄ ❄ ❄

Squeeze the lemon over the apples and pour the honey over them, tossing them lightly. Combine flour, brown sugar, ginger, allspice, cinnamon, and ground cloves in a small bowl, stir, then sprinkle over the apples and toss lightly.

❄ ❄ ❄

Take 3 slices of bacon, cut them into ½-inch pieces, and cover the bottom of the pie crust. Place one layer of apples over this, along with 4 small cubes of butter. Continue layering the pie with one slice of bacon cut into ½-inch pieces, apple, and butter cubes until the pie is a mound, topped with apple and the last of the butter. Cover it with the rest of the dough. Be sure to make slits in the dough. Place in the oven and bake for 30 to 40 minutes. Let it rest for an hour before serving. Enjoy!

Photo by Paul DeLuca

CHAPTER SIX

Pie Tunes, Playlist,
Children's Books About Pie, and
Great Pie Fights in Movie History

PIE TUNES PLAYLIST

Here is a compilation of upbeat bubblegum pop, big-band swing, bluegrass, country, doo-wop, jazz, and rock songs that celebrate our favorite dessert. It's a family-friendly playlist for your pie contest pleasure. One could create an R-rated version, but I'll leave that to you (and if you do, don't miss the 1990 heavy metal classic "Cherry Pie" by Warrant). Another pie song that I love, but that's a little melancholy for a party, is "Making Pies" (2002) by Patty Griffin.

"Apples, Peaches, Pumpkin Pie" (1967) by Jay and the Techniques

"Bake that Chicken Pie" (1930) by the Jackson County Barn Owls

"Blueberry Pie" (2002) by Hoi Polloi

"Blueberry Pie" (2005) by Orange Sherbet

"Buzzard Pie" (1947) by Rudy Green and His Orchestra

"Cherry Pie" (1997) by Big Jay McNeely and Dana Gillespie

"Cherry Pie" (2010) by the Go Find

"Cherry Pie" (1986) by the Jayhawks

"Country Pie" (2008) by Fairport Convention

"Eep, Ipe, Wanna Piece of Pie" (1940) by Fats Waller

"Honey Pie" (2000) by Lavay Smith and Her Red Hot Skillet Lickers

"I Can't Help Myself (Sugar Pie, Honey Bunch)" (1965) by the Four Tops

"Key Lime Pie" (2005) by Kenny Chesney

"Mom's Apple Pie" (1991) by Tyrone Davis

"Petootie Pie" (1946) by Ella Fitzgerald and Louis Jordan

"Pecan Pie" (1996) by Golden Smog

"Rhubarb Pie" (2004) by John Fogerty

"Rhubarb Pie" (2008) by Five Iron Frenzy

"Rhubarb Pie (Hot Commodity)" (2002) by the Laurie Berkner Band

"Shoo Fly Pie and Apple Pan Dowdy" (1945) by June Christy

"Sugar Pie" (2004) by Har Mar Superstar

"Mudpies and Gasoline" (2004) by Patricia Vonne

CHILDREN'S BOOKS ABOUT PIE

To get children excited about your pie contest and/or to entertain them as festivities wind down, I recommend the following kids' books about pie. All are recommended for ages four to eight.

✳ *Pie's in the Oven* by Betty G. Birney. Published by Houghton Mifflin in 1996. A boy spends the morning with his grandmother as she prepares and bakes apple pies.

✳ *Pickle-Chiffon Pie* by Jolly Roger Bradfield. Originally published by Rand McNally in 1967 and reissued by Purple House Press in 2004.

A three-nosed Snozzle creature with fuzzy ears and an orange polka-dot necktie makes pickle-chiffon pie.

* *The Blueberry Pie Elf* by Jane Thayer, illustrated by Seymour Fleishman. Originally published by William Morrow and Company in 1959 and reissued by Purple House Press in 2008. Elmer, an impish little elf, gets into the blueberry pie and swoons with delight till he eats too much.

* *Easy as Pie* by Cari Best, illustrated by Melissa Sweet. Published by Farrar, Straus, and Giroux in 2010. A boy is inspired by his favorite TV cooking show to make peach pie.

GREAT PIE FIGHTS IN MOVIE HISTORY

Not to give you any ideas, but the following movies contain spectacular pie fights.

* In *Bugsy Malone* (1976, rated G), directed by Alan Parker and starring Jodie Foster and Scott Baio, gangsters fight with pies and shoot guns filled with whipped cream instead of bullets.

* *The Great Race* (1965, not rated), directed by Blake Edwards and starring Tony Curtis, Jack Lemon, and Natalie Wood, features one of the biggest and silliest pie fights ever filmed.

SELECTED BIBLIOGRAPHY

BOOKS

Carroll, John Phillip. *Pie Pie Pie: Easy Homemade Favorites*. San Francisco: Chronicle Books, 2005.

Clarkson, Janet. *Pie: A Global History*. London: Reaktion Books Ltd., 2009.

Dimock, Anne. *Humble Pie: Musings on What Lies Beneath the Crust*. Kansas City: Andrews McMeel, 2005.

Haedrich, Ken. *Pie: 300 Tried-and-True Recipes for Delicious Homemade Pie*. Boston: Harvard Common Press, 2004.

Le Draoulec, Pascale. *American Pie: Slices of Life (and Pie) from America's Back Roads*. New York: Perennial, 2003.

Segan, Francine. *Shakespeare's Kitchen: Renaissance Recipes for the Contemporary Cook*. New York: Random House, 2003.

Struthers, Jane. *Pies: Recipes, History, and Snippets*. London: Ebury Press, 2008.

Swell, Barbara. The Lost Art of Pie Making Made Easy. Asheville, N.C.: Native Ground Music, 2004.

WEB SITES AND ASSOCIATIONS

The American Pie Council—www.piecouncil.org

The Food Timeline—www.foodtimeline.org

What's Cooking America—whatscookingamerica.net

ACKNOWLEDGMENTS

*Pie is a symbol of many good things because pie, whether you are
baking one or eating one, is rarely a solitary occurrence.
It is a social experience, a way to bring people together. Pie is rarely
eaten alone, except maybe for breakfast the next day.*

John Phillip Carroll, cookbook author

. . . .

This may be a little book, but it carries within it the goodwill of a great many
people.

Pie folks don't just talk about community—they forge it at every turn,
and I am grateful to the kind souls who so generously shared their pie wisdom
and cheered me on as I worked on this project.

It's been a pleasure working with my publisher, Andrews McMeel. In
gratitude, I offer Apple Pie à la Mode to editor Dorothy O'Brien, market-
ing whiz Amy Worley, designers Tad Carpenter and Holly Ogden, publicists
Tammie Barker and Razonia McClellan, copy editor Michelle Daniel, and the
rest of the crackerjack team. For Jean Sagendorph of Mansion Street Literary
Management, S'mores Pie and she knows why. And I hereby award blue ribbons of thanks to all of the pie contest winners who gave me permission
to publish their prizewinning recipes.

A toast with Key Lime Pie Martinis to my pie mafia sisters: pie judge extraordinaire Lesley Ann Beck, author Mollie Cox Bryan, food historian Janet Clarkson, food bodice-ripper writer Shelley Handler, Ruth Hanrahan of the Pie Town, New Mexico, Pie Festival, Arlette Hollister of the Iowa State Fair Pie Contest, Linda Hoskins of the American Pie Council, Beth Howard of theworldneedsmorepie.com, Tricia Martin of the Pietopia Pie Contest, master pie baker and teacher Kate McDermott, Mary "Pie Lady" Pint of American Blue Ribbon Holdings, Kat Selvocki of Piety Bakery, Ellen Spear and Laura Wolf of the Hancock Shaker Village Country Fair Pie Contest, Sarah Spitz of the KCRW Good Food Pie Contest, Dana Tommasino of Woodward's Garden Restaurant, and Betsy Usry (and her swell husband, Bob) of the Smithville Chicken Pie Festival.

For my intrepid interns, Peter Fitzgerald and Errin Patton, slices of Grasshopper Pie, and for Jennifer Pelzman, a stranger who dropped everything one weekend to help me fact-check pie songs, Sugar Honeybunch Pie (I made that up). My home slices, Anne Burt and Susan Davis, and my mom, Leigh Hyams, have my back as ever and they deserve Chocolate Bourbon Pecan Pie.

Eternal best wishes for perfect crust to my pie recipe–testing posse: Amy Bass, Monica Bliss, Lauren Bufferd, Paul Clark, Paul and Renée Mills DeLuca, Nichole Dupont, Debra Ginsberg, Sharon Jandrow, Millie Rossman Kidd, Karen Lee, Ericka Lutz, Carole Murko, Kari Chapin Nixon, Paige Orloff,

ACKNOWLEDGMENTS

Lisa Peet, Peggy Reeves, Jean Sagendorph, Lynn and Jason Sherwood, Linda Waterfield, and Karin Watkins.

And for my sweetie pies, Dave and Annalena Barrett, a promise to learn how to bake Grandma Babs's Pumpkin Pie.

TALLY SHEET

DESIGNATED NUMBER	CONTESTANT NAME	TYPE OF PIE	SCORE
1.			
2.			
3.			
4.			
5.			
6.			
7.			
8.			
9.			
10.			
11.			
12.			

ABOUT THE AUTHOR

Gina Hyams is an author and editor whose Nebraskan grandmother baked killer apple pies. Gina served as a judge at the American Pie Council Crisco National Pie Championships and has published several books on family traditions, travel, and the arts. She lives in the Berkshires of western Massachusetts with her husband, teenage daughter, and dog named Goose, and she lives online at www.pietakesthecake.com.